Mapless in Underland

Also by Melinda Smith and published by Ginninderra Press
Pushing thirty, wearing seventeen
First… Then…

Melinda Smith

Mapless in Underland

Acknowledgements

Many many thanks to my fellow 'Mull 'n' Fiddle' Poets Martin Dolan, Suzanne Edgar and Michael Thorley for sharing their responses to early drafts of many of these poems. Thanks also to the poets and tutors at the Five Islands Press January 2004 Wollongong Workshop, and to the curator and participants of Conversations: Art and Text exhibition at Goulburn Regional Gallery for their inspiration and feedback. All imperfections that remain are my fault alone.

Acknowledgements are also due to the following for first publishing poems that appear herein:

Muse, where 'Waiting for the Sun', 'Stir' and 'Sur Vive' (shortlisted for ACT Poem of the Year 2003) first appeared;

Chas Eales (Community Broadcasting Association of Australia) for broadcasting 'Bright side', 'Trio', 'Not writing', 'Red velvet afternoon' and 'A simple twist' on his *The Words and Music* radio program;

The Society of Women Writers NSW Inc. for shortlisting 'Bride and Best Man discuss arrangements' for their 2003 Poetry Prize and for publishing it (as 'Infidelity') in their anthology *Sharing a Landscape: a celebration of difference* (2003);

Composer Sandra Millikien for setting 'Waiting for the Sun' to music (available from SULASOL music publishers, Finland);

Five Islands Press for publishing 'Stems' in the Wollongong Poetry Workshop Anthology 2004 *My Cat Cannot Have Friends in Australia*;

Suzanne Edgar for including 'Virginia Woolf' in her talk about that writer given at The Edwardians exhibition at the National Gallery of Australia, March 2004; and

Goulburn Regional Gallery, for displaying a number of poems in the Conversations: Art and Text exhibition in June–July 2004.

Mapless in Underland
ISBN 978 1 74027 264 3
Copyright © text Melinda Smith 2004
Copyright © cover image Catherine Swarbrick 2004

First published 2004
Reprinted 2015

GINNINDERRA PRESS
PO Box 3461 Port Adelaide SA 5015
www.ginninderrapress.com.au

Contents

Losing things	9
Trackless	11
Trajectories	12
Stems	14
Broken record	15
end face away ring hand said	16
Stirring	18
Light	20
Wheels	21
Diocletian's Palace	22
Dereliction of duty	23
Mother Love	24
Virginia Woolf	25
Sur Vive	26
Heat	28
Wanting Things	29
Stir	31
Force	32
Waiting for the sun	33
Unravelled villanelle	34
Bride and Best Man discuss arrangements	35
Guilt haiku	36
Food	37
Introspection	38
A simple twist	39
Untitled	40
Winnie Blues	41
Evillanelle	42
Triptych	43

Finding Things — 45

- Inspiration — 47
- Chain mail nightmare — 48
- Consequences — 49
- Alikasudara — 50
- Sappho — 51
- Mary Kostakidis — 52
- Cold — 53
- Turning — 54
- A group of poets: the collective noun — 55
- Tableau vivant — 56
- Red velvet afternoon — 57
- Glamour travel — 59
- Far shore — 60
- Art — 61

Dedication

For my family, friends, Michael, and Samuel

Losing things

Trackless

You'd think I'd stop bringing
road maps on these river journeys
but having the wrong
scheme of the wrong things
terrifies less
                    than drifting
without coordinates
here, where all paths ever taken
are equally hidden
and the waters forget you
as soon as you pass over.

Trajectories

A corker in her day,
at twenty she struck sparks
from a young engineer.

He hooked her
telling the Bridge's story
– the spidery, swaying halves,
their tenterhooks mid-air meeting:

north shore, south shore and a lucky arch.

They married in June. She followed him
down to the raw uncertain Snowy.
That first winter nearly finished them
but by the next one
they had knuckled down to things:
taming rivers, raising sons, saving for a farm.

The day they took possession
of their prized Monaro acres
was their seventeenth anniversary.
He thought he might run for mayor.

They never expected the stroke.
Doc took her aside:
'His limbs are useless, love. Reckon
you'd better learn to drive.'
It felt like being mugged.

Near the end
he sat in the kitchen, staring,
loose change scattered on the placemats.
He looked at her.
'Gawd, Dot, I'm frightened now.'
He fingered the coins.
'I don't know what these are.'

He hated her having to feed him.
His hand locked over hers,
from table to lips
the spoon made a trembling arc.

Stems

This autumn
for the first time
I heard the leaves falling.

A sound like soft drops of rain,
or the pad of secret feet through grass.

Once
I heard brittle stems
screaming as the wind dragged them
in their hundreds
over a metal roof.

Broken record

Why, lover, did you let me get away
with that? It should have been more than enough
to make you snap and send me on my way.
Why, lover, did you? Let me get away
– some things a man should never have to say,
and I won't say them now. Just call my bluff.
Why, lover, did you let me? Get away.
With that, it should have been more than enough.

end face away ring hand said

The man tiptoed in late and slid into the end
of the second-last pew. Nothing showed in his face
as he watched the proceedings. He did turn away,
come to think of it, during the bit with the ring,
when he seemed to be rubbing his temple. His hand
looked all clammy from clutching the program. I said

to my uncle, 'Watch that one.' He nodded and said
that the bride had some pretty strange mates on her end.
Then he grinned, and by snickering into his hand,
camouflaged his guffaw as a cough. The gilt face
of his watch told a quarter to three, as the ring
of kids armed with confetti formed up. 'We're away!'

yelled the groom. As the tulle-laden cars pulled away
trailing several photographers, somebody said
that they'd almost begun to despair of a ring
on *her* wandering wedding hand. Later, the end
of the smorgasbord queue gossiped on, but the face
of the mystery guest was a blank. 'Gotta hand

it to him, bit o' guts to show up.' The bride's hand
fluttered diamonds and gold, but his eyes flinched away
as he strode to the 'out of town' table. Brave face,
braver handshake. Aunt stared. 'That fling's over,' she said.
'I dunno,' Uncle wheezed through his cigarette end.
'I'll shush up. Hope John kept the receipt for that ring.'

'Wash your mouth!' hissed my aunt. 'And at least Tracey's ring
is a real one!' She flapped a plump, age-mottled hand
in his face. His eyes crinkled: 'I've kept up my end
of the deal, diamante or no: kept away
from temptation – "forsaking all others", they said,
and I did. You're my missus for good.' In his face

there was something like tenderness. Aunt made a face
that said this had been gone through before, but her ring
made her smile as she flashed it at me. 'Enough said.
Lucky me.' Uncle winked and took hold of her hand.
'Come and dance, darl. We'll blow these part-timers away.'
So they left me there, wondering how it would end

for today's bride. Her face was smile-wreathed till the end
of the night. The last ring formed to clap them away,
while outside, someone said, a glass gashed a man's hand.

Stirring

The year I was fifteen
when the Show came to town
I went all on my own money.
I won at the laughing clowns,
had a whole fairy floss
to myself
and went on the gravitron
without throwing up.

Walking home afterwards, I left my girlfriends
at the corner,
headed uphill alone to the rectory.
The grassy side of the street
muffled all footsteps: the first sound I heard
was a whump between my shoulder blades.
Hot, shocked tears
stung into my eyes.
I whipped round, wheezing.
Rolling at my feet:
a half-eaten apple.
Twenty steps behind:
the Year 10 boys in a mob.

I could still feel the apple
in my back, a spreading
target-shape of stunned skin.
> 'Hey, priesty-girl. Goin' ta church?
> Run home and cry to Daddy.'
Lava rose in my chest, hotter
even than tears.
My mouth opened
every swear word
I had ever learned
spewed from me
piling up
with the apple crumbs on the ground
until I was knee-deep
in filthy
glowing
four-letter
coals.

The street went very quiet.
Fifteen bum-fluffed jaws
dropped into the silence.

Light

Old Parliament House (side view)

Clean lines of classic
deco white barnacled with
air conditioners

Daylight saving

They're brightening up –
all the worn faces heading
homeward in sunlight.

Bright side

Two gaunt pensioners
pause on the long, grey footpath
to point at gardens.

Wheels

As kids we poured our smart-arse scorn
on the four-foot screeching Dalek hordes
because a single flight of stairs
could stop the whole invasion dead
in its little rubber-tyred tracks.

We're older now: the jokes have stopped.
Instead, we're clamouring for more tar
to pave our way to glory, for
at sixteen, humans grow a car
and never leave the road again.

Present us with a mountain now,
deprive us of our wheels, and watch
our jelly legs, our blubber arms
struggle and fail. The Dalek curse:
we can't go where we cannot roll.

Diocletian's Palace

At the edge of an iridescent gulf
called Adriatic, called Jadran,
white colonnades, four storeys high
make aqueduct faces at the sea.

Inside, in a stately octagon,
Greek columns at the corners, lies
the Emperor Diocletian. Tiger-
size obsidian sphinxes guard him.

One wonders if he got the joke
when a later empire of Rome
raised an eight-sided cathedral
round his Christian-killing bones.

These days, three thousand Croats make
hives out of his palace walls.
The young men, bereft now of their war
are ominous in leisure suits.

And underneath the massive arch
where tributes were laid to honour him
two bearded Iowans discuss
their camcorders, their children.

At the edge of the iridescent gulf
called Adriatic, called Jadran,
white colonnades, four storeys high
make aqueduct faces at the sea.

Dereliction of duty

Felt a poem coming
like a sob:
tight air in my throat;
crying ache in my jaw.

I was too tired to catch it.

I turned off the lamp
breathed out
and let it go.

Mother Love

Wave after wave, the ocean counts the cost
by piling sheets of water on the sand.
I dreamt before your birth that you were lost.
I think I have begun to understand.

By piling sheets of water on the sand
the sea offers its body, slice by slice.
I think I have begun to understand.
I love you knowing sorrow is the price.

The sea offers its body, slice by slice,
heaving itself onto an empty beach.
I love you knowing sorrow is the price.
I start a task whose end I'll never reach.

Heaving itself onto an empty beach,
the sea still finds the energy to give.
I start a task whose end I'll never reach.
I give you life, not knowing how you'll live.

The sea still finds the energy to give.
I dreamt before your birth that you were lost.
I give you life, not knowing how you'll live.
Wave after wave, the ocean counts the cost.

Virginia Woolf

Inspired by the abstract portrait *Virginia Woolf* by visual artist Kirsten Farrell

Veiled in muslin,
intellect like a steel ribbon.
Reaching up for new words, you fought the weight of your father;
grappling with the old rigour, energy, dominance,
insanity. You pored over the Odyssey as a girl,
never suspecting the birds would later sing to you in Greek.
'I meant to write about death, only life came breaking in
as usual.'

Was it death, or life, dragged you under?
Ouse was the name of your last river,
Ophelia's your grand gesture:
lying white as lilies on the bottom,
failing, like sunlight over empires.

Sur Vive

The trees are trying to forget
but their bones are black with remembering.

It came to us on a sunny Saturday:
on the day of golf games
at the hour of weddings.

Out in the forest the fires had joined forces,
gathering to a mob of flaming brumbies
ridden hard by a hell wind
straight for the suburbs.

Hundreds of burning havoc hooves
thundered through the backyards of the innocent.
Black smoke ate all the light;
at three the sun went out.

It can be hard to think of much at all
up on the roof
blind in the stinging wind
dribbling the garden hose into the gutters.
But you know
hearing the rushing sound over the hill
you know
feeling the wall of heat slam toward you
you know
diving from the path of the orange cannonball
you know
shoving Mum into the car
you just know
squealing the tyres
bricks are pretty heavy but a life weighs more.

That night we met our neighbours
camped near us in the high school hall.
The smoke smell would not leave us.
Slowly we felt our way
along both edges of a new belonging:
knowing the people in your street
by what each of them has lost.

Heat

Signs & Wonders

Spring drought. Swollen clouds
cough their raindrops down as dust:
brown powder manna.

Ash Sunday

Saw a smoke-black bloke
grin the raw news down the line:
'Darl, we've lost the lot.'

Wanting Things

Stir

You stir me up.

You're a night storm
far out to sea.

Come morning,
       you've churned
              my calm sediments
                      to a gritty mist;

changed my colours;
       chafed my ripples
              into surf:

my muscular, unfamiliar breakers
roar in like horizontal cyclones,
       dumping surprised bathers
              face down in new rips
                      on my weed-strewn beach.

Force

Do we really have to keep apart all night?
or year? or life? I'll slip. You magnet me,
my iron-filing cells all wrenched one way.
I'll fall. This aching blood, this bloody ache's
near bursting my calm skin – apply the cups;
incise my inner arm, and drain me off.
Choice is the word of nightmare. Wake me up.

Waiting for the sun

I am a sundial
in a sunken garden.

On the days when you show your face
I bask, all those long warm hours.

You only see me when I glow,
borrowing your radiance –

but behind me, where you cannot see,
circles a cold shadow blade.

It gets longer the closer you are to leaving,

and in it
are all the iron-frost memories
of the days when you do not come.

Unravelled villanelle

I nearly stopped and spoke to you today
but piked at the last minute in sick fright
I couldn't think of anything to say.

I don't know why I'm still running away
I've hidden from you since that awful night
I nearly stopped and spoke to you today.

You'd think that I could get a grip, and stay
and make at least some small talk, glib and bright.
I couldn't think of anything to say.

ay
ight
I nearly stopped and spoke to you today

ay
ight
I couldn't think of anything to say.

ay
ight
I nearly stopped and spoke to you today
I couldn't think of anything to say.

Bride and Best Man discuss arrangements

They lured each other down onto the beach
with sidelong ripple-whispers and the light
but tidal tug of Truth or Dare. (Hot night,
cold water). Crossing dark dunes, they were each
too hypnotised for speech.
Lace shallows closed around their ankles. (Trapped).
A forearm grazed a hand, unleashing lust
full-lunge. The straining anchor lines all snapped
and left them grappling in the surf. (We must…
we mustn't…shit, we just
have). All the galaxies convulsed above;
infinities of ocean foamed and hushed
by turns; then they were done. Lucky enough
a hiker sprang them, sparing them the rushed
and usual lies (blah love,
blah sex). Push come to shove:
his death-by-drowning nightmares soaked the bedding;
she dreamed of one more go before the wedding.

Guilt haiku

At the bonfire's heart
the flames make bright, shifting walls
for hot, black chambers.

Food

Meat

The cattle truck's full –
an inside-out skeleton,
flesh in wire bones.

Trio

Three at the table:
one innocent smile facing
two guilty parties.

Introspection

(homage to Bob Dylan's 'It's not dark yet')

It's morning again
and I'm still looking for you.

I wish I could stop
but I can't make myself want to.

I follow you in full light
when I close my eyes

but I wake up alone,
my bed all covered in lies.

A simple twist

(homage to Bob Dylan's 'Simple twist of fate')

When I asked you to cross the line
it was just an idea of mine
in a head too full of wine
to think what it would mean.
Now, knowing where we've been
I know not what I do
skating on a river full of you.

I'll have to pay for all this lying.
Curse this crooked life of mine:
doing good most of the time
and evil when I can.
I might call myself a man
but I keep on slipping through
the ice above the river full of you.

I lost my wisdom, I lost my sense,
I'm close to losing all my friends
and it makes no difference
that you don't care for me.
I can clearly see
the end I'm coming to:
drowning in a river full of you.

Untitled

My love, she lies a-sleeping in a far-off bed
on the far side of a mountain that I cannot climb.
But every night I dance the dance I'll dance the day we're wed
and every morning swear that it's the very last time.

My love, you cannot see her by the light of the sun.
My love, you cannot touch her with your noonday hands.
My love, you cannot find her till the hourglass has run
and the sleepers start to walk upon the fallen sands.

My love, you cannot catch her in your net of wine.
My love, you cannot hold her in your chains of smoke.
You can see her in the mirror when she starts to shine:
speak and she will disappear into the words you spoke.

Now I'm calling for my love across the shadow land,
calling out her secret name all lonely nightmare long.
But my love, she seems to be content to leave things as they stand:
my love, she makes no answer to my shadow song.

Winnie Blues

Spare a thought for your Winnie Blues, now you be givin' up smokin' again.
Oh have some mercy on your Winnie Blues, now you be givin' up smokin' again.
They just been givin' you simple pleasure, and you gotta go treat 'em like it's a sin.

Well, you take 'em out your fav'rite pocket, and you shove 'em in the drawer of shame.
Yeah, you rip 'em out o' that there pocket, and you ram 'em right down in that drawer of shame.
And they be trapped there under the gas bills, a-cursin' all over your name.

But when the full moon come round again, you get that itchin' in your hand.
Yeah when the time of trial come round again, sure 'nuff you get that wanderin' hand.
And you go a-riflin' through them gas bills just as fast as you can.

Could be true what they been sayin', them Winnie Blues'll be the death of you.
Hell, you been sayin' it you own self now, them Winnie Blues'll be the death of you.
Best get done with them cigarettes babe, 'fore they gets done with you.

Evillanelle

You cannot see my evil in my face
– no use to lodge it where it cannot hide –
my evil lies in quite another place.

The dark lines are more difficult to trace
though many came before you, boy, who tried.
You cannot see my evil in my face.

You may consider this a special case
but all your searching looks will be denied.
My evil lies in quite another place.

Observe the sly spell working in the space
between what's right and what is justified.
You cannot see my evil in my face.

Watch, as desire achieves a kind of grace;
salvation lies in being satisfied
– my evil lies in such a slippery place.

Locate it if you must: find the black space,
or try to run – but know you cannot hide.
You cannot see your evil in my face.
Your evil lies in quite another place.

Triptych

For all the dark dawns	For all the hours	For all the madness;
you made me pass;	of giddy heat;	all the fear;
for all the lies	for all the days	the promises
you made me tell;	of empty hope;	I had to hear -
For all the times	for all the months	for all you took
you made me ask	we'll never meet	that I could not give –
which one of us	and all the years	I hate you. But
would go to hell;	I'll need to cope;	you made me live.

Finding Things

Inspiration

The orchards drop their blossoms
on last year's apple-buckets
and here am I, stuck
scrabbling
between muddy roots
for water.

Chain mail nightmare

Dead again, it seems I've come back
to drift along these ceilings. Frere
Valentin's still dragging his sack,
his lover's corpse inside. I dare
to stop him – I must know, I swear:
'Answer me! Will we be here long?'
Silence. 'Speak! Will we be here long?'

His stare has pity in it. 'Ask
the children.' Down below our feet,
a group of youths at table. Ask
I do – they cannot hear. I beat
the walls; spill wine, and snatch their meat
to spell my question out. They flee,
wild-eyed. No one will answer me.

My heart sinks as my form floats back
to drift along these ceilings. Frere
Valentin's still dragging his sack,
his lover's corpse inside. I spare
my question – perhaps I will care
but little for the answer: 'Long.
We will both be here very long.'

Consequences

Olympia!!

Come to me now
pretend
that I'm Cher in *Moonstruck*
and you're my mother

Do that great scene:
'Look at you!!! Your life is going down the toilet!!'
Shriek that this sorry mess
is my fault and no one else's

Lay into me
Olympia
with all the wrath that rumbles in your mountain name.

It's only you will do, Olympia:
hell can't scare me
Jesus is too gentle
and as for Jiminy Cricket –
well, he lit out at the first sign of trouble.

Alikasudara

It's Glendi time. We're all Greek for a day.
The makeshift stage is creaking as it fills
with boys in spangled waistcoats. As they dip
and spin, and stamp new shoes upon the boards,
old men are keeping time with farmers' hands.

The music pulses out across the grass.
Beyond the deck chairs, saris in a group
are picnicking. The wearers clap along
and then, made bolder by the sun's effect
on retsinaki, stagger up to dance.

As men with dark moustaches take the hands
of laughing aunties swathed in red and gold,
an ancient conversation starts again:
the waistcoats on the stage shout 'Alexander!'
the saris answer 'Alikasudara!'

The aunties on the grass dance out the tale:
the honey-skinned Invader from the north.
The quick feet on the stage sing of the quest
that won the Indus lands, but gave them up
soon after the great General took his rest.

Praise accidents of history. These eyes
meet here again across a flag-decked park
-among the mingled smoke of barbecues,
the tang of sunscreen and the breathing grass-
still dancing on the bottom of the world.

Sappho

Inspired by the abstract portrait *Sappho* by visual artist Kirsten Farrell

Sex still draws us into your scattered fragments.
All your hot young lines with their smudged-out endings:
petal-tatters clinging to swaying bodies
pulsing flushed and pink with the tease's power
holding all our heads under scented, cresting
oceans of aching.

Mary Kostakidis

Inspired by the abstract portrait *Mary Kostakidis* by visual artist Kirsten Farrell

Most people miss it: they see
an autocue reader with a pleasant face. I see a goddess
radiating mystery: eternal
youth singing with the wisdom of sybils.

Knowing what you know, at
once you tell all, and keep
silent, laying bare
the souls of the scrolling words
as all our suns set: daily prophecy, hidden in a
kind of hymn.
In the next life, you will be the herald of
day and night, love and war.
In this one, keep bringing us close to the truth, for all our sakes.

Cold

Foliage

The bare oaks rustle
their black and white winter leaves:
restless currawongs.

Below average

Cold summer. Warnings
to rug up. We hide indoors
from the wind's ice edge.

Turning

It's started. The first wood smoke of the year
smudges the chilly air – the piles of logs
have only really started to appear
since Easter. Foot-thick early morning fogs
muffle the lake: white sheepskin over glass.
Leaf blowers prowl nut-gravelled paths. Thoughts turn
to corduroy on afternoons the gold
of sun on poplar leaves. The children learn
that last year's gloves don't fit. Their parents pass
whole days hand-washing jumpers. Frost-tipped grass
makes the poor yard look like it's getting old.

A group of poets: the collective noun

A frenzy of poets
A rapture of poets

A draft of poets
A concentration of poets
A mull of poets
A fiddle of poets

A line of poets
An anthology of poets
A smattering of poets
A broadcast of poets
A lexicon of poets
A stanza of poets

A school of poets
An order of poets
A stable of poets
A faction of poets
A pride of poets
A herd of poets
A battle of poets
A bed of poets

A muddle of poets
A gabble of poets
A chorus of poets
A catcall of poets
A sozzle of poets

An oxymoron.

Tableau vivant

London. February.
A bitter Tuesday
stalled between stations on the District line.
I can see my breath in the carriage.

Out the window
on Wimbledon Common
the morning promenade is passing:
sets of two-legged silhouettes
bulking under arctic wear,
each set leashed to a four-legged friend.

Heads are hunched against the wind
but tails are waving free:
busy flags and pom-poms
adorning a mute march
against all Februaries, all Tuesdays.

Red velvet afternoon

It's Simply Barbra tonight.
The whole table opposite is men. Short hair. Nice aftershave.
They've made sure of prime position by the stage.

On the PA
Edith Piaf implores 'ne me quitte pas'
for the fourth time since lunch.
The wait-girls are at the darkening windows
closing the curtains:
gold rings click softly as the velvet moves under them.
The walls are the same glossy red; the room
seals us in: a plush imprisonment in a box of Valentine
chocolates.

I've been nursing my Earl Grey all afternoon-
shirking work and watching
the cavalcade of faces in the wooden booths.
They've all been here: the rock-climbing club;
the girls' monthly catch-up; real-estate bores; baby's first outing;
an awkward accidental meeting; the end of the affair.
Each hour new groups sliding along the benches,
families in the pews of an all-day church.

Most have trickled home again now,
deaf to the entreaties of Piaf.
The night service draws a different crowd.

I think I can see Barbra on stage
arranging her music:
a clean-cut young man, jeans and white T-shirt,
with a serious mouth – the lippy will come later.

The coffee machine cranks up a forty-espresso whine;
a clash of plates crescendos from the kitchen.
The punters must be fed before the lights go down.

I didn't come for the show. I slip out
into the dark. No moon.
The hike across the oval takes forever.
Feels like the sun has set for good.
Looking back, there's no sign of life
but a small ruby glow from under the mountain
and the faint opening bars
of *The Way We Were*.

Glamour travel

In the circle of hell called 'transit'
infinity is a carpet
the signs are in no language
and all air is conditioned.

Here Qantas laid my Sunday
on the International Date Line rack
and stretched it, sobbing for mercy,
out to forty hours.

Far shore

Virginia rustles with strange trees
caught
in white nets of highways

Art

Offcuts

Salon floor sweepings:
all the sleek-headed stories
have this other side.

Not writing

Even fishermen
must keep ashore, some days, to
mend their precious nets.

www.ingramcontent.com/pod-product-compliance
Lightning Source LLC
Chambersburg PA
CBHW062202100526
44589CB00014B/1912